Song in Tammuz

"*Song in Tammuz* gives us a lyric voice that speaks—no, sings!—back to tradition, sings with devotion (to a 'god attached to the end of your name / like the tail of a mare'), yes, but also with questioning (and whose letters are 'the last telegraphs to be sent before the city surrenders'). There is grief, yet awareness that as she writes, 'a last good lemon hangs from its tree.' There is an incredibly memorable persona, Ruth, both mythical—and our own. There is a story of horror sewn out of silences, out of the unsaid. And, always, there is a song: 'first anger, then hunger. Then song.' This is a marvelous first book."

—Ilya Kaminsky

"Avia Tadmor is looking for new names for home. *Song in Tammuz* is stunningly tuned to the frequency of loss—loss of beloveds, of homelands, of identity born of place. These songs are steeped in her suspicion that 'love works like any language…we utter what we can't reach' but keep trying to, with the 'perpetual hunger of dogs.' Tadmor's speakers, who straddle centuries, echo each other's migration and displacement, and include the Biblical Ruth, in whom we might find ourselves, 'know[ing]…that each stride onward, there will be more & more to lose.' Yet across generations, these voices are humming with a commitment to live, to forge new loyalties, to make lives built from love even when it is scarred by distance. This collection of poems, and this poet, so honest in her assessment of how loss 'burns through us,' keeps me reading and returning, reading and returning. The language of longing, of an urge for intimacy despite the 'terror of being alone here together,' is tuned with such precise attention it brings solace. Tadmor's collection reminds me that poetry, in its willingness to pay such attention, enacts love—miles and oceans be damned."

—Farnaz Fatemi

"'We utter // what we can't reach but spend our lives / reaching for.' This reaching-for gives *Song in Tammuz* its quality of deep embodiment, illustrating how a body that is singularly in the world is also a representative of other minds, hearts, and voices across time. Bringing together story, memory, and history, Song in Tammuz reckons with how the present is always weighted by the past. With our current moment so darkened by crisis and grief, Avia Tadmor insists on a countervailing dignity and illumination. 'Her pen is a stronghold, a lighthouse.'"

—Rick Barot

"Avia Tadmor's astonishing debut, *Song in Tammuz*, examines biblical and contemporary explorations of identity, power, and desire, but desire here doesn't seek to occupy but rather enjoin with tenderness and care. This formally dexterous collection takes us on journeys across deserts and cityscapes, centuries and continents. The centerpiece is a striking, innovative series made of numbered blank pages with footnotes at the bottom, which reflects erasure and embodiment, annihilation and resilience, and acts as loving tribute for a grandfather who was the sole member of his family to survive Auschwitz. Family, friends, lovers, and readers are invited to enter visceral, sensual, full-bodied worlds. These are rapturous and necessary poems that alight."

—Hadara Bar-Nadav

"In conversation with the biblical Book of Ruth, Avia Tadmor crafts a brilliant exploration of displacement, migration, and loss. *Song in Tammuz* merges the identity of the speaker with the character of Ruth, both women seeking to be known, both seeking the holy and the whole—in geography and intimacy. The poet uses form skillfully to contain memories of lost homes and the desire for new homes. Elegiac, ekphrastic, and definition poems explore presence and absence while beseeching some higher power: 'even now, see me asking compulsively / for a newness, a promise / however unshapen.' From a grandfather in pre-Holocaust Czechoslovakia, to Ruth's famine-stricken migration from Moab to Judah, to the speaker's move from Israel to the U.S., horses, crops, land, rivers, and light provide a language that binds old and new. Tadmor eloquently captures the paradox of exile: '... Although I am countried and housed / I remain stupefied in my journey / on most days / still searching for home.'"

—Ellen Bass

Song in Tammuz

Avia Tadmor

T P
Tupelo Press
North Adams, Massachusetts

Song in Tammuz

Library of Congress Control Number: 2026939746
ISBN: 978-1-961209-69-5 (paper), 978-1-961209-75-6 (eBook)

Cover and text design by Howard Klein.
Cover art: Lauri Hopkins, "Fertility Totem." Used by permission of the artist.

Author photograph by Beowulf Sheehan.

First paperback edition October 2026

Tupelo Press
P.O. Box 1767
North Adams, Massachusetts 01247
(413) 664-9611 / Fax: (413) 664-9711
editor@tupelopress.org / www.tupelopress.org

Tupelo Press is an award-winning independent literary press that publishes fine fiction, non-fiction, and poetry in books that are a joy to hold as well as read. Tupelo Press is a registered 501(c)(3) nonprofit organization, and we rely on public support to carry out our mission of publishing extraordinary work that may be outside the realm of the large commercial publishers. Financial donations are welcome and are tax deductible.

Table of Contents

למשפחתי

for my family

by the fire of those who came before—
to you, who are here now

It's like a lighthouse, except that, as one swims toward it, it backs away.

Louise Glück

Exodus Song

When the drowning comes, know
there are still horses, loose and alone
in the old country— their eyes flipped upwards,

the horseshoes snapping one after the other and shooting
into the great black night like Delilah's
headlong blades. When the drowning comes, know

the farrier will rebuild his shop, sell toys
or trinkets on an avenue decked on both sides,
he would notice, with unfamiliar flags. But the horses—

they will be running and running until they are no longer
horses. The bare hooves will lift and lash
like decades dusting a country

with wet black ash. Remember it even then, underwater:
the warm rush of blood, the old heart, its pulling
and plunging the way a woman's gullet

pulses the psalms. Remember the boy watching
his teacher on fire, how her body relights the city's
ghostspun square. A girl already in her new country

reads Dostoyevsky in English. Her hair smells of mothballs
and basements, walls discolored with rain. She moves
her pen in the margins, a tongue

not yet her own. *Have I been grateful here? Was I driven by purpose?*
And were these always my own thoughts regarding the afterlife?
Her pen is a stronghold, a lighthouse

flickering late in July. *Did I make it a home?*
Did my brother feel pain? All my life I am trying, Lord,
not to inscribe your full name.

Ruth \ ˈrüth \ (*n.*)

Meaning *friendship*. Meaning f*light*
of rare birds. Meaning *a woman*
who doesn't belong here. Meaning I wanted
to know, when Naomi, meaning my mother-
in-law and friend said, *go to the threshing floor.*
When he sleeps, uncover a place at his feet
and lay there, make yourself known
meaning *seduction*   *what else*
do you have, did she mean
to define or defend me?

Night Will Soon Fall on the Lake

The hour the sky repeats the color
of water, no difference between what is lit
and what is reflected. By the neighbor's dock
I see the black dog again, his unlikely body
rising out of the water—massive, mythological
creature with hair like ruffled feathers.
I leave my wine glass on the deck
to join you inside. Upstairs the skunk's spray
had drifted through the bedroom window
and you have a hard time believing
in skunks. You, who grew up in a skunkless
country, are surprised you like it. It reminds you
of fertilizer and hash. Yours is a faith that leans
on earthly proofs. I lie down beside you.
We have been spending the summer
in another couple's bed. No longer newlyweds
so why does each day still feel like a plunge
toward discontent? The grill you said you'd clear
of the snakes, dead and tangled
as lovers, but didn't. The inexorable whirr
of the bedroom fan. Even the god
you shut yourself to when the nurses cut
your father's wedding band with surgical pliers
and whom I can't stop asking to singe
my dark edges. Even on my wariest days, I unbutton
myself and ask, in my greed, *make me different,*
make me more. From back home we hear
of your oldest friend, now twice separated.
Of my sisters who nurse second newborns,
then third. As though they are light years ahead,
it's impossible now to catch what they say
through the phone, goddam fan, and who is to say
if we're getting better at any of this. Just once
I want to be like you. To be able to settle
for the earthly proofs. Now, it is August. I know

what you think. I am harsh, I give too much
or not at all. Whole mornings I could sit silent
out in the open shed amidst the green starts
of what we assume are tomatoes. My fingers feeling
the prickly nubs or my finger holding, for hours,
the same place in a book. Up here, so far from the city,
far from the countries where we were born
by now in another millennium where each year
fewer of our loved ones are still alive,
nights are biblically cool. When I press
my stony feet to your shins, you give me
some of your heat and I know it is something
of your heart. Yours is a secular warmth.
Outside the rain starts again and I can tell
by your silence that my gripping won't do
for apology. Under the sheets we said we'd wash last night
and didn't, it isn't apology you are after anyhow.
I worry, love. I don't know what we've been after.
All I know is I can't help myself if tonight it is cold
and your body feels massive. I want to say
black dog massive. I want to say something
that rises from under the water. I want us to speak
of the terror of being alone here together. Of the dog,
its slick, distressed feathers. How its faithful muscles
move above bone, its thin legs that tread
with incredulous lightness on the marshy ground.

In the Tongue I Was Born To

the word for husband
means owner, for wife means *woman*
and woman, *man* housed with *god*

which is to say, I hear him some mornings
stirring among the leaves in the garden, restless
as every animal gone too long

unsatisfied. Which is to say, we can't always localize
anguish, but I know the smell
of semen, how it wafts from the carob tree,

pods packed with brown pulp and seeds. I know
what he tells me: chemists would sell the ripe fruit
to singers so their voices would be soothed

by which he meant, some of me could learn to like it.
Some of me is thinking of war-women, how they press
vinegar-rags into wounds

to survive them. Some of me says survival is seeing
only the peak of our wake: him, strangely-
angled and high-pitched; me in my sudden hunger,

the old glass factory swarming with gulls— one of us quick, the other one
quicker, both of us stunned, as all dying things
by desire fading out unevenly

which is to ask, how holy is holy, how can I be a man
housed with god when this union,
this tongue, this poem even, has failed me, what good

are the gulls, is the man, are the words
are the singers, their gullets
this morning, unhousing in me—

Lemons from Levant

.א

If I carry my father with me
it is in my name and the scent of cypress
in my hair, thick as sheep's wool
against the shearer's blade.
It is in the two veins that run down
my forearms, blue asps, rivers
Phrath and Hiddekel. They empty
into whatever I'm writing, even now.
Because Lord, you have kept the seasons
turning, made the salmon float back
toward the gulf, up-turned
but gleaming like pink confetti.
And because as I write this
a last good lemon hangs from its tree.
Say you have made it so, Lord,
that you meant it. Say there are riches
in ruin. Say, who lied to you.

ב.

Once, I knelt for a New York man
and he grabbed my hair
like a bridle. His knuckles, a colosseum
of bone. He grunted
some other name, mistaking me
for relief from the cold, for a home
one builds for one season
and because I was lost
in this new alphabet, I scoured
the letters as if they were the last telegraph
to be sent before a city surrenders—
the soldiers frozen in various positions
each twisted on his own sword—
but I could not carve my own name
because in English there is no letter for god
and because in this country, some forms
live longer with no sound.

ג.

What is it to have a Semitic god
attached to the end of your name
like the tail of a mare, whipping
with protest at every step she takes
through the blonde grass?
You will not ask what it means
to be here, you only know
you have not come this far
to wear the torn shoes of the dead
and stand in the rain in a thin wool coat
squinting at house numbers.
And that you, like the mare,
will kneel forward some day in tallgrass
or like Ruth in the yellow fields
of Judah. Like that, yes, you will kneel
for a stranger. You will kneel to be known.

Ruth Before Leaving Moab

Tonight, I imagine all the women who walked away

from this city of stone

& into the wilder embrace—

how they bore themselves,

clay carafes

brimming with rainwater & how they too

had known fear, felt its airless flutter

as I do: filling the throat like live birds

bunched in a smokestack before a thunderstorm

because they know—

the same way they know the season

for breeding from season to roam—

that each stride onward, there will be more

& more to lose.

Afloat

Summer and Lara and I tell ourselves
we're poets, we're writing
even when we're not *writing*, which means

we spend whole afternoons swigging the nips
her husband gave her for advent, hitchhiking
to Sweet Briar Lake

where today she offers to teach me how to swim
or float—clearly I can't do either. And she is a good
swimmer, Lara. On weekends her dad

would carry her and her brother at 5am
from their beds to the car, drive almost three hours
to Assateague—that's how much water healed him

after her mother left. After breastfeeding
her daughters, Lara's boobs never shrank back
which is why she is buoyant—motherhood

keeps her afloat, literally. I know what she means
though it's hard to take her seriously
with her polychrome goggles, blue and emerald

dragonflies take turns catching themselves
in her eyes. Lara mentions Freya, Norse goddess
of dragonflies, lust, fertility. When I try to see

myself in her gaze, I can't. Summer
and I know I look graceless. My strides, more spasm
than swim. Lara explains it's my own

weightlessness that exhausts me. She's right, I'm all skin
and breastbones and I miss my body, the curves
the depression had stripped away

those frostbitten months I've struggled to separate
love from compatibility. I drift on the steadiness
of her instructions, *lean back, ears in the water*.

She had a really good Jewish friend growing up
and what's that prayer you say in the all-women's water?
She means mikveh, I think,

but I'm not that kind of Jewish. I've only been once
before my wedding. All I remember
is a Yemenite woman, blind in one eye,

peeling loose strands of hair off my back so I can be dirt-
free for my new husband, clean
even of what my own body makes.

Back at the dock Lara asks,
do you mind if I change here? I don't
and her swimsuit thuds against the wood, heavy

with lake water. She wants to know
what I'm writing about but goes on to answer
and I feel relieved. She's writing about Demeter,

the deuteragonist of the story. For years
she could only see herself as the daughter,
Persephone: her mother gone, her sex drive

steering the story, driving her toward all kinds of men
from hell. But now she's fifty and nobody's
daughter. Our stories

like seasons, turn. I turn
to ask her about the pomegranate
but now we're up close, she is naked

except for her Norse Goddess goggles— indigo, mint,
my face constellates in the sky
of her face. We are impossible not to see.

Ruth, *oil on canvas, Francesco Hayez, 1835*

Looking at you I know I am a woman
who looks at a woman

crossing a field from across
the dimly-lit centuries

and still, I want to traverse the longitudinal

pleats of your garment, stitch
purpling under your partly-

bare breast. The same way I want to stroke

the sheaves that spill
from your half-hidden hand

as if they were the sum
of your misgivings: each stalk

innately split, a self.
Looking at you, I worry

that as soon as I turn away, you will drop them

onto the dream-colored ground. The pulse
in your wrist spasmodic,

unthreading, I am a woman

who stands and looks at a myth
of a woman who stands

between two rivers, amidst a blur of trees

or black smoke. Unsayable
is the way

we desire—
or should I say, *I desire*

you, the image of you, facing-not-
facing me facing you.

Touch has a memory.

John Keats

Campanology

The first time I went down on a woman
I thought I invented it. I wanted to patent it,
you said after you left the religion, stepped

on the night train from Schopfloch to East Berlin—
in your black plastic bag you swaddled a bottle
of Fanta, the braided butt of day-old

raisin bread. Your one holy possession—
a German-English dictionary,
which you promised to one day return

because you were raised to revere
what is not yours alone. You didn't say
if the hole in the sheet was a myth when I asked,

or if it's true that we love more intently, wholly
after having kept time-honored distance, from a woman
or god— you didn't say

but I understood both the sheet
& yarmulke were reminders that love works
like any language, we utter

what we can't reach but spend our lives
reaching for. *I want to ring the lone bell*
in the back of your throat, you'd tell her

as if you were climbing the blue-
domed church in Santorini on the hottest day,
thumbing the cool caper buds, tomatoes

yellow & green on their vines—what grows wild
after long desolation. *I want to ring the lone bell*
in the back of your throat, you'd tell her

suspecting, it isn't the chiming we want
    but the echo. What shapeshifts & stuns, then stays
        burning through us—

Ruth Remembers Imagining the Foreign Field Before Leaving Moab

It's true, I hated the thought
of the women who left this hillscape before me—

their bodies that rivered past sheaves, smoke-stirred
shadows, their voices

pulsating like summer rain.

My body
had always wanted another

but most nights I dreamed of them laying alone in the clearing
belonging to no one. I imagined

soles that grow thick until splitting open,

insects lay amethyst eggs
in openmouthed sores. I hungered

to know what winged thing breeds in the flesh
or how by the end of a season

something turns into sawfly or moth. It was spring

and I washed alone, watched cane toads at night
eat their own, so by summer

I'd wake up forgetting—
the songs of the tribe, the stakes

that hold the temple. To be free

of the seasons, of living thankful, to be free
even from god. I trusted the old world

will reassemble without me,
but could I trust the inarticulate

music— its faint tymbal
in my pulse?

My Grandfather Delivers a Survivor's Testimony at Yad Vashem but Does Not Say Auschwitz

My first name was Adolf. My father,
my mother, what did they know?

From the German, meaning both noble
and beast. Meaning they trusted I'd live

unafraid my roots could be showing,
less worried that someone will see through

to the part of me
longer than my own life.

I have three names, four tongues, a place
behind my heart where I carry

my earliest dead. I was fourteen.
The ID my father's friend forged for me

said I was a Catholic farmboy. Meaning I'd learn
to bury the parts of me that I had once

named my life. On Sundays, I'd join
the old couple in church. Under the sign

of the cross, I'd survey the pews,
boot-marks on every floor tile.

I was a boy. My sister, my brother,
my parents, their parents,

were ashes in October sky. Other Sundays,
I'd imagine the altar-side foyer

leads to a stucco-tiled kitchenette
where my sister sits, peeling lemons.

Or I'd imagine all of them feeding
on pine nuts out in the snow. Or that they were

the snow, crowning
the Tatras. I turned sixteen

on the refugee boat. The ID I found
when we passed through Marseille

said I was married, had fathered
two sons. The first time I held

a Jaffa orange I made a promise: to stay
forever close to land. I studied

phytology, developed a strain of peanut
that can be grown in the cruelest drought.

I knew what hunger was. I didn't know
there are parts of a man that are reborn

with each of his daughters. Mine, three unscathed
coins I'd hold up to the light

with mud-covered hands. If not love, what I felt
for the ground-nuts

is kinship: the fruit must grow into itself
wholly underground. I don't know how long

before a new geography becomes a home.
Maybe only when you have daughters

who know there will be a permanent plot
of earth they could visit one day, trace

your name on the granite and sing
their grief for you. I chose my new name, Abraham.

Meaning, between beast and nobleman,
I don’t trust either, and I knew sacrifice.

I still don’t know lucky from fated. Or what
is deserving. What I know is I lived.

Ruth One Year After Leaving Moab

Some days I can't do anything but remember
hinged gates

choking with bands of wild garlic & the habitual

motion of cow mouths

stuffed the whole afternoon
with ripe tomatoes & silage. To be snared

by the reliable rhythm—ox hooves press

week after week into mud, hefty music
of bodies doing work through a life

they did not choose. But how else to live?

To make room for the stars, which give light
still from their displaced dominion

in the water well? My father, he'd clutch

& lift them, break the day
brisk with his bucket. The metal resounds

in the mind like a prophet & his congregation:
it rings once

& then once more. All my life I've been told

I am greedy for loving this earth
not when it yields, but after—

when it is made again large with hollows—

even now, see me asking compulsively
for a newness, a promise

however unshapen, whatever

will be next year's meal—

After the Bad Year I Want Things to Be Still

so I fixate on the shapes we make on the glass: two
stenciled outlines against a fast-flashing scenery. Light
lashing a lake, another lake cindering through
a doily of dogwoods. In Beacon, the train slows at last. Bird-bellies
brush over a quiet life. Fishing boats cribbed
in the harbor. A wind-whacked American flag repeats like a jingle
on every other dock. Since Poughkeepsie
we have not said a word but we are eating Doritos
and passing a bottle of Diet Coke metronomically
between us. On the ticket, my name is inscribed
next to yours and I know that we chose this ride, its quickfire
impressions of cornfields, rickety bends. This whole trip
you've been typing away on your laptop,
and not without reason. October's rent bounced
and your mother, wakeful by a different ocean, forgets
more of her words. Still, why do I want you so badly to notice
the branches, scraping-not-scraping the window, harsh
but harmless like the hands of our best-meaning ghosts? Or the inlet
committing itself to the Hudson, the Hudson prayerful
toward the Atlantic, saying *yes I surrender*
to your larger surge. I lick the orange dust off my fingers.
So often this year I craved nothing more
than to be suspended entirely in the hour. Perhaps like Monet
that day on the beach in Trouville. Camille's gaze averted,
Monet squeezing blues straight from the tube
to eternalize the dark underside of his new wife's
parasol. Sand and traces of shells blow on the canvas,
rapid white streaks for the Normandy light
consummating her skirt. Ahead, our own city
inks into shape against a bruise-colored sky. The narrow space
outside the restroom is a buzzing hive. The space between us
is me pretending to daydream, digging up one more
Dorito. I'm all will and want. A tongue, unrepentantly
orange. I want you to look. I want you to see how I burn
for every bit of this dust.

Here, No River Flows So He Names the Village Oasis

Father Bruno Hussar, Founder, 1972
Oasis-of-Peace – Wahat al-Salam – Neve Shalom
واحة السلام – נווה שלום

A hut, a cot & a window overlooking
the olive groves

needleworked through the valley. A desk
from which to pen my vision

for the village-to-be: this hilltop,
a no man's land—suspended

in the armistice lines
between the West Bank & the god-sworn silence

in Latrun, where Trappist monks
turn rough dirt in their vineyard,

replanting what the season's
wildfires consumed & it is a love

so soundless
it intoxicates. Here on the hillscape of biblical

bloodshed, the wind blows dry-
mouthed. Barren,

it tunnels through wreckage & ruin, jawbones
of beasts rein over the rubble

for centuries. Forty years
I traded belongings. A childhood in Cairo.

A youth in Paris. Once a trained engineer
& a Jew, I am a priest

of the Dominican order. Like any good convert,
I know newfound faith

lives in proportion
to whatever doubt came before.

A man of the book, I write *peace*
like any type of devotion

must take shape in language first. Consider a triangle:

(A)
Arabic اللغة العربية

(B)
Hebrew עִברִית

(C)
English

As to say *Lord, let peace stretch large over this village, a white canopy—*
three-pegged & equally trued
to each of your people's tongues.

Or to say *Let this place spring as a spiritual centroid,*
god's word extending from these
coordinates equal distance to:

(A)
The mu'azzin's call for Salat
in Ramallah رام الله,
hurled into the evening
under the mosque's green light.

(B)
In the Hebrew month of Elul
a woman commits Tevilah טְבִילָה, a
purification by the seaport in Tel Aviv.

(C)
Jerusalem
القدس
יְרוּשָׁלַיִם

In every language I speak to god, I ask
what does it mean for a land

to be promised? Lord, for any *promise*
to hold on this hill,

let it live like the word—
as part of *compromise*. Like Isaiah's

word, *the wolf also shall dwell with the lamb*
and the leopard shall lie down

with the kid. At night I lie down
with the coyotes & listen

to the first families' fireside singing,
alternating guitars

& darbukas, Yiddishkeit
& Umm Kulthum. The village's first child

stands primal over the valley
in sand-stiffened sandals, undershirt

blotched with sun. She howls into the wind, a howl
that resists

any one grammar & is therefore full
of possibility.

Listen—

how wildly
it conjugates toward the unscripted sky.

Self-Portrait in Virginia, Facing East

I shut the screen door and descend

the stairs from my studio. Limp-legged,

a black wasp continues to cling to the mesh.

Five days, she has not moved. Last night

the resident writers were doing shots of tequila and talking

about this country's depression, our students' depression, and how it differs

from our own. *Teachers can't show it,*

Lara said, which made me think about the Latin root, *deprimere*—

how it means to press down, though for me it's been more

the sensation of being untethered; the pounds I've been dropping

all year, slick oil from a skillet, unstoppable

panic attacks like mid-sea vertigo. Now, I wake up and can't comprehend

how is it already June? Last week, the southern storms

tore down two aspens but this morning the world seems more legible

even if it is not. I cross the lawn; half mud, half meadow.

The barn; weathervanes rustling *east and east and east.*

I'm thirty-five. I've come here pill-stuffed, unchildrened.

When I face east all I see is a row of paint buckets

where the groundskeeper is growing her weed

under a camo tarp. I don't see her at first but she's gesturing

come on over, she has beers and she offers to show me her

woodshop, it was the old stable, the garden too if I want.

I don't know why I feel like crying when we pass the tidy beds

with endive, rutabagas, tomatoes, and beets—bursting

with such a disquieting purple I think of placentas,

radishes so libidinous that even this minute I think

of birth. When my husband calls

to tell me the new coffee machine arrived, I feel ashamed—

how clearly I know: I never want to leave.

Artists come and go, she says, *but only someone as rootless*

as me is good to actually live here. She straightens

a fallen tomato vine like pulling a hair from a pillow, presses down

the trellis, the soil around it, to fix what the storm had done.

From up close she looks like she's pushing sixty. I'm not sure

why she invited me over, or why when she says

no money no children no church, it sounds like a tease

or humble-brag. I pass my beer bottle back and forth

in my hands, nervous-clink on its torso with my

wedding ring. It's hot. I don't always trust my choices.

Ruth from a Sudden Clearing in the Foreign Field

I forget where Dibon is. Forget
where Edom is. Barefoot I cross rivers
Arnon, then Nimrim. My feet make sounds

the banks had never heard. Twice, I remember
my father and do not know
what to do with my heart

or with the Phoenician tongue,
my Moabite Kingdom: I carry it
broken inside me, perpetual

hunger of dogs. At night in my makeshift bed
under the great acacia, Judean winds
pluck leaves off branches. Like tongues

they taste a world tasting like ash,
like the old country that keeps spinning itself
around the mind— a blanket

of limestone hills and barren plateaus,
the youngest ewe born hoofless but nursing
through winter, snow falling

even in spring. At night, the old women
who raised me return, knitting
in my own voice to warn me

against my insatiable heart.
And the heart? She tilts, heavy-
antlered, like the great acacia's roots.

Dirge with Humming Desert

after Traci Brimhall

The last time I saw my brother, he'd been dead
eighteen months and came as a ghost in the passenger seat,
his arm hanging out the window and whistling

an old boot camp song. He said
we were born on the two ends of Tammuz
and that our grandmother, ever since Dachau, knew God

wanted us close. The road curved along the Hasbani River.
He turned his head toward the apple groves, let the wind breathe
on his beard as if it hadn't been

washed and treated in Tahara. Cursed the plains,
their magnificent light in the Arabic he'd learned in a village
beyond the plateau. We stopped for gas

and he took off his shirt. Shrapnel gleamed like mussel shells
caught in the skin above his ribs. He said he'd travel again
underground, spend nights counting beetles

in trenches, that he'd tasted the blood of palm trees
in yellow dates on the other side of the drought.
Years ago, we saw a woman with wild hair

pull bits of gold from her mouth and cast them
into a sinkhole by the Dead Sea. Flies bustled
in and out of her dress. The desert hummed

underneath like an engine refusing to cool off.
When the sun vanished into Jericho, she chanted something
in Russian, bent over to watch the last bit of gold

overcome by a womb of earth. The rim collapsed
under her weight and hours later they mined her,
dogmatic, unwilling to show herself

through muck and salt. No one claimed her. A tourist,
my brother said, and he held me so I could stand
what the land, in its unquenchable thirst, had done.

Writing to You

Here it is August, already
the fall webworm is busy

weaving its bridal tombs
in the poplars. My hair grows long,

it will gray & I worry how soon
the first sunlit arrows will shoot past

the dogwoods & into the bedroom
window, the one facing east.

Again, I will not have written to you.
Look, even now

I've written this line & stopped
to put on the kettle. Already day

unrobes its pale torso & it is the way
the night rider's horse tends to water: veined neck

leaning toward what a moment ago,
could only be supposed.

All I can do is suppose where you are,
this morning, I mean. This hardly-

mauve minute. When I think of you
it is always your sunburn-red hair

which comes first. It is always three weeks
before the war that would call

both our brothers. Your body not yet
at war with itself, we'd never

horsebacked so close to the border—
past the shirtless men who fish

along the Banias, past the boys
teaching each other to burn

the glochids off prickly pears.
How is it that all I've been teaching myself

is to hold what punctures & burns
at a distance, that we must canter through hurt

guardedly & on our own? On our way back
from the horse ranch

your car broke down. Remember
how we swerved into the ditch? How it burst

with wildflowers? The engine stopped
& our girl bodies started

shaking with fright & fury,
then laughter: how summer, as if it knew

all we were going to lose—had won us
this unwritten time.

Lucie Last Summer

for Lucie Brock-Broido

in Cambridge

I biked to your grave   brackish breeze

my sweat

rubbing against someone else's

on the rental bike   I thought

of the velveteen coat

you bestowed me   said it paired well

with my *heelhood*   those years I did tread

high-booted   sure-footed

daily seduced   or seducing someone

through the linoleum corridors

of Dodge Hall

you'd say   *delete not dilute*

& speak of how spooky

the path we all tread

murmurs & apparitions   along it

this practice of solitudes   reaching

for common solace   five years

& still I feel the warmth

of your fire brass candelabra

clenched against a nightgown

high-necked & rustling

in that Victorian way

how high your candles

lit & carried us

through the cat-slick dark carry us still

toward what words

we find in ourselves on equinoctials

you'd gather us close

write toward the terrible crystals—

yes it was spooky to be alive & sailing

together in language

even more spooky

the rhapsodic rattle of language

that keeps you here

Ruth \ˈrüth \ (*n.*)

As in gnawing distress, as in sorrow
for one's own sins. Probably two women
in a field beyond town. They lay
for days on the unshorn bales.
Their breath tells of barley
and wheatgrass. All they want
is to float without falling
between sky and dank earth,
to say each other's name
as if it were a hymn
for solstice, the reprise pounding
through them even in sleep.
But now, both are awake. They move
in hunger. Hands crossed over
bare breasts, theirs is a hunger
that has been spinning inside, hung taut—
a dimly lit chrysalis, likely
for centuries. *I am not like you*,
one opens and closes her eyes on the other
like saying, *I have meant to be meek*
and fear my own failure. Above them
birds migrate south. They drift
on the upwash of one another
and do not have language for it.
From the east, the sun spills
on the slopes. How does god want them
to drink in such warmth
knowing it will be what ends them?
Probably with eyes shut hard, mouths
newly awake and tongue
retracted. They know it's a sin, though it feels
like every animal kneeling—
blood-pumped, it hardens
into new speech.

A mountain keeps an echo deep inside. That's how I hold your voice.

Rumi

My Grandfather Shows Me the Sepia Photograph Tucked in his Passport Pocket but Does Not Say Auschwitz

[1]

---

[1] The boy you see in this picture is not me but a figment. When I appeared, it was late in my life. This boy was born to a woman with arched eyebrows and a much shorter man who was hardworking, exact. Every morning, the woman would cut two yellow apples across the equator to show her children how the seed pockets make four small stars. I imagine the boy's younger brother, Tuvia, chewed quickly before he'd run back outside. I imagine the boy's sister, Malka, spellbound by the ceremony of it: granular shimmer, seeds. She had the same lips as your mother, except for a thin scar on the left. The family owned a sugar factory for a few generations and there was an unmarried aunt who lived with them or not far away. They had more than one dog and a small chicken coop in the back. There was a cornfield, and I imagine they were comfortable. I imagine none of this meant what they thought it meant.

2

[2] The boy you see in this picture is not. He is a story. The son of a woman and man who made their living from sugar. They read Polish and German, prayed in shul, took their children to swim in the Poprad. They were austere. Practical.

[3]

[4]

[3] In this picture, there is clemency. The family is posing in front of the house, the mother seated in the middle on what must be a narrow stool. Underneath her, the shadows of three slender legs cast themselves on the ground. The father, you carry his middle name, stands on her right. His hand, large on the boy's shoulder, large for a man so short. It is the hand of a man that will say to the boy, *you must turn away from this.*

[4] The boy in this picture is not me but a figment, a fog. When I appeared as you know me, there was no god and I had to make my own. Every time I began, I was skinless. Every time I begin, I am drifting, inexact.

5

6

[5] Imagine the dust at the corners of schoolbooks, the heels of their days. Dust they collected in peacetime games. Since you ask, their favorite game was Children of Wolves: born and raised in the forest. In summer, they'd cover themselves in dry mud, weave their hair with acorns, pine-twigs barbed between their teeth. And if winter, they'd do the same in their ushankas and boots. Three different sizes, but cut from the same piece of buckskin.

[6] Imagine them thinning. Imagine them stripped to the bone and what of their feathers. What of the acorns, pine nuts, twigs. I suspect those were the only things they took with them. What they kept coiled in the heart's first wool.

7

[7] There were prayers for flood, sleeplessness, orifices, dead cattle, heart failure, nights with no stars. But prayer demands exactitude and expectation, both of which the boy forgot. His first music also escaped him. The slam of the screen door, the icicle touch of the locks. The tallest birches traced his footsteps, the mud. And there was a girl, a friend of his sister, whom he had to forget when he was on the refugee boat and they assigned him a wife, twice his age. What he remembers is cornfields: locusts scratching inside his head. The loud. The loud. The loud. His sister, her name was Malka. When he looks at your mother, he remembers her lips, the sky around his brother's face. He doesn't want to forget them, but every time he begins, he is drifting. The impossibility of memory being exact.

8

9

10

---

[8] *You must turn away from this.*

[9] In a recurring dream, the boy overhears his mother and father talking about whether to sell the sugar factory or the house. They're afraid it won't be enough. Could there have been enough. And he has a feeling, this is only the backstory. His name is borrowed. So is his tongue.

[10] This boy will learn to live in the days. For the living, he will bury his dead every morning in the empty *domovy* of his mind. At night, he will join them. Lead them to the curb of the road, into the cornfields beyond, and away.

11

---

[11] The boy you see in the picture is a breath in the cold. When I appeared as you know me, it was late. I was taller. I had been reborn bereft of story. I have been writing it since.

12

[12] In that one dream, he cracks open a window, unlocks the pink tongues of cows, then climbs on top of himself to see himself scurrying away through the overgrown corn. Both his hearts pounding. Both his hands and his chin wet with November. The family, from its early end of the field, keeps calling his name, their voices shooting across husk-shaped shadows. Or their voices call and he must call himself back.

Through the ear, we shall enter the invisibility of things.

Edmond Jabès

Ruth Twelve Years after Crossing the Water

Once, there was another field. I would go there
in summer. My grassland, my feet
caked in earth.
                                        The sun ripened in the navel

of cumquats. At night, the stink of goats and hyenas
rose and fell in no particular measure
as if it were borne from the moon.
                                                    As if to say, soon—

winds will chime from the fells
of a different country. Like asps
they will move through you.
                                        Let them. What split tongue

they will brush cool against you. Be willing,
be alone. Obey the strange hiss
they will bring to your lips,
                                                    lines from a scripture

you did not know. But its music—
the way it will override language, drown out
a need to know.
                                        Like a shepherdess

surveying a turf at a distance, her voice titanic
and sprawling through the unhoused night.
And the night itself,
                                                    how it tilts

over the turf, over the flock's
belled scruffs, the animal hearts traveling elsewhere
through the thin edge of sleep.
                                        And because it's the way

you too will move after the field,
when crossing the water. And the way the water
has always moved through you—

nights with faith, nights without.

My Sister Carrying Her Darkness Like Silver

Summer was already standing
with her in every room. Its new fingers

running against the long edge
of the kitchen counter, the pool's just-painted lining

and springboard. Summer followed her
throughout our cousins' house,

leaving behind the warmth of an animal's body
in grass, the animal of her

reaching already and always the question
of children, the animals of children, how do they live.

When my sister climbed onto the springboard,
water sparks scattered

in haloes behind her. The cypresses stood
thick in their green; our cousins suspected nothing.

The girl gone now and I am thinking
what must it have been like

to be ill and rising, what soar
precedes the sinking. When my sister jumped

off the white-lacquered board, she was a child's body
passing a row of neighborhood condominiums:

each house like our house,
cluttered in its small evening and dimmed

in its own way. But when she rose out
of the water her hair was black

and long, silk spun
by the Jewish weavers of Bukhara.

She cut it. Her braid lay, a black calla
on the bottom of our cousins' pool.

Tonight, I see it from the distance of rainfalls
in another country. A small figure

carrying her darkness like silver, tight-lipped
and misspelled. She looks into the eye of her torturer

as if beauty can only be beauty
but the night, her night, will not give.

From my sister I learned,
madness takes the blameless

and rids them
of their most graceful possessions first.

October, her hair grew again. Slick,
undirected, the first fur

of animals. I was thirteen. I told no one
how an evening cluttered with footsteps

is only the ill-lit dance
of the lost. About the girl with thin wrists

dragging the night by its terrible antlers
through her attic bedroom

until sorrow blossoms red peonies
between the wooden floor boards.

Then it was winter and I told no one.
The peonies sprung, shock of red

feeder-roots—
first anger, then hunger. Then song.

My Grandfather Returns to His Birth Town in Now-Slovakia and Remembers the Music

Dear Kežmarok

I was all of you   the house & its injured   rafters I was the lone birch   that grew
where we buried   my sister's first teeth   I was the neighbors' boy   his one
good eye & buckskin slingshot   April   the finches would crash   into the
schoolhouse windows   fold under their own squeaky wings   I was their wings
& the barn   where my family scurried   when the soldiers paraded   starved
hounds   shadflies   scattered like November cinders   What were you Kežmarok?
In the dream I keep returning   & you are the viola   someone goes on playing
as they are led through the birches   & told line up   line up by the ditch   dybbuk-held
you play on   you do not lose your pitch

Ruth Seeing a Herd of Wild Oryx on a Hill in Jericho

Now if I carry my mother with me

it is the way she stood by the hinged gate
the summer I strayed

into unsung swards. Afternoons
she would toss bread at pigeons

& nightlong stitch my sisters'
wedding veils. It is the way her fingers bled

honey from blisters. Her eyes, I have them, Sumerian
olives—mine pitted, hers full

of god. What I carry now is the weight
of that honey. It is the hefty plough, chisel

& hardened share of that god.
Of my sisters, alive by their own motherhood,

they flip black braids
from one breast to the other & newborns

suck the air, a native search
for comfort. There is no comfort

here in my near-fifth decade of living, my breasts
give nothing. Sun-parched figs. I was supposed to

die like ryegrass, like a plant that clings
to the ground. To be buried one day in Moab

beside the women who raised me—

Nothing Promised

You drag the boat across the tallgrass, shake out the black snakes that made a provisional home under the bow through the length of winter. The rope undone for the first time in months, it slews behind you through dirt, then shallow water. A thin trail that follows you deeper into the afternoon, submits to the pull of you, or perhaps the pull of the other shore. So sure you are in your solitude, and I am startled to sit here, witness it. How smooth is your sailing away, this measured but steady drifting under pink, penumbral light. When we first met, you portioned your stories or they came brash, a light tower's unpredictable beam. Resolving to muteness the year your father could no longer hear you, then woodwork, then a decade of travel. Tulum. The Mont Blanc, where the five-foot two French guide hauled you out of a crevasse. The Norwegian girl you met at a bar in Cambodia, who followed you back, wanting to show you the ring on her labia. Her Janis Joplin tattoo. I follow you now with my late summer eyes. Why do I love watching you like that, cruising away from me? As if you are teaching me something about love and distance. Two red-tailed hawks surrender their shadows to the thicket of spruces. You stare up, then past your left shoulder. I think, at me. The wind tugs at every boat in our world, a hushed push and pull, a measure of faith travels the distance between us. Buoyant as day, thin as light.

She is Three and to Her This is Just the World

Her mother forever dancing
to Gloria Gaynor, gutted bell peppers sliding
like afternoons from her palms into pots

and there is only one day: Saturday.
On this Saturday, we walk to the beach.
When I buy her ice-cream, she plucks

the sprinkles expertly. Each time
her finger lifts up, she offers me one more
balloon. We pass an occasional jellyfish and I say

hurry up, Alma! Let's get back to the shade!
She agrees, but a few feet later we spot a whole
lifeless bloom. They are funny.

An expert again, she starts counting
one through eight, then ten, then giggles,
leaps to thirteen. Now she wants me to count

from the beginning to the very last number in the universe
and also to pet them. When she says *pet them*
her head tilts back and I marvel at how sharp

are her canines, tyrannosaurusly long and made
this particular way to tear through flesh, the sinewy heart
of anything living.

Little fish-eater, little carnivore. How she dips her halo
of curls into daylight under a blazing sun.
The lifeguard passes by where she crouches.

He asks, *is she yours* and I say
yes, yes she is mine because her mother is far enough
I don't think she can hear. And because

I'm a coward, I know, to claim motherhood
while giving up nothing, while having done nothing
but move my tongue.

The lifeguard's voice vaporizes
into megaphonic omniscience, instructing two boys
to swim away from the breakers—

this minute, he says. This minute I think
of the Zen teacher who counselled my pregnant friend
to accept she's becoming both more

and less of herself. Of my sisters, reporting how
motherhood changed them when I asked if it made them
more or less afraid to die. I am afraid

of the tide, its galactic pull. I am afraid I've already
wasted so many years because I've been both unsure
and late in every choice I made. And I am afraid

of you, Alma. Of the benthonic water
inside you. Your feverish body, a boatful of want
as you arch over the jellies, pink-rimmed bellies

filled only with brine. The whole of you shimmers
with sand and I envy you, the way you know
in your bones— you have nothing

but time. That you've been here forever, and never-
astonished, sliding through stars
or licking your way past lichens. The sea?

You have guzzled its spume from your palms.
The sun? A seeded musk-melon. You're here to assert
as long as you can, your numberless greed for it all.

Ghazal from an Ocean Away

What I know of war I had learned in my first country, in my first tongue
and on my first beloved's body. I can say it through the distance of this other tongue.

He'd release all he learned about war into me. The fan droning above, he'd hold on to the
headboard as if it were the titanium ledge of his world. If he kissed, he kissed with no tongue.

His first weekend back in Magdiel, he drove to a friend's tattoo shop, asked for a horse silhouette
on his upper arm. He said that he was its mane, and he was on fire, hellburnt black tongues.

In the field hospital, he made me a blood bracelet from an IV drip tube. He sealed it with
his two good fingers, watched the strays lick it with pink, thorn-strewn tongues.

You can say it, Avia, in your faraway tongue: Say night sweats. Say eyelids that will not shut
in full sleep. Say the fan, say its droning inside him. Inside you, this tongue-hungry tongue.

Oh You Bruised Your Knee She Says and the Truth is I did Not

even notice suspended as I am
in this blue chair and poised
as a grasshopper clung to the underbelly
of grass Oh you bruised your knee
my gynecologist repeats and apologizes
for this will take just a minute in which I will
feel mild pressure and in that moment
I want to tell her of all the bruises
I've ever suffered hell I want to
tell her of all the bruises my sisters
have suffered the ones that go on
even now as she is easing the pressure
on my lower abdomen repeats
this will take just a minute although
it must have already been five but I say
no worries I say I don't mind I imagine
the grasshopper's belly which I remember
is where its ear-like membranes
are carved I don't think anymore
of the doctor before her who praised
my bone structure how he joked I am beautiful
on the inside and now one after the other
she peels off her gloves purple and white
they change color each visit her clogs too
I never noticed the music they make
or her mask which lowers a little as her eyes
at last meet my eyes and this is assurance
by which I don't mean being naked or bruise-
kneed in front of another I mean
it's astounding just thinking about it
my belly my bones or her belly her bones
how all of us really were carved this particular way
by which we can be entered and held
really held from inside

Ruth on the Third Day of Mourning

for H.

Naomi/

why would you let me/ behold you

blank-eyed & empty

of light at the end/ already untethered

from this earth & unable

to receive/ what I say—

my larynx/ a cricket's wings

inconsolably rubbing

to make the hymns/ you loved most?

Did you mean to show me

that if I sing in this world

as long as I can/ I will not be spared—

as I was taught to believe

from my own ruin?

Or perhaps/ you meant to give me a sign—

here at the end

of my fourth decade

& seeing/ that although I did

marry/ although I am countried

& housed/ I remain

stupefied in my journey/ on most days

still searching for home? Perhaps

you wanted to teach me

this much: our final song

is not/ the lone plot of earth

where we are brought to lay

at the end/ it is not

the immovable rock

lain above it/

no it is only

the migrating light/ that which scours

the fields/ & refuses to stay

in one place

as though you meant to say/ yes

yes we persist

in the day's afterglow/ the whole cricketed

earth/

incarnadined

In Gratitude

She is not a complainer, my friend. We walk along
the Jackie O reservoir, curve along its wide pelvis,
eastbound hip. She recounts, as a matter of fact,

her chills, shivers, heat waves, what she can
or cannot eat. It's the first sunny day in April, first Sunday
since her surgery. We cross the park from the west

to the east side of the city. Sweat dripping
down her forehead, she smiles at everyone we pass by,
or I think she does. For months I've had to complete

the rest of her face in my mind underneath the mask: her beautiful teeth,
spray of moles that climbs up her cheekbone
like ivy. Let me show you something, she says

and takes a sharp turn past the cherry tree boulevard
where couples pose under bridal canopies
and the ground too, heaves with blossoms.

My friend disappears into a small dirt path
and I follow. We are far from other people. Here, we can
peel off our masks, move from one airlessness

to another: the manurial mulch, fresh rot, and I see it—
a small flower garden—except the tulips
have not yet opened, they don't even look like tulips

with their sealed off crowns, spearheads cleaving upright
through the dizzying air, vortex of wet bark and pheromones
as if cutting through whatever the virus,

the unending frosts, the whole of last year
did to us. My friend is glowing now. When she says *tulips*,
she rolls her *L* as if to remind me: we each learned

to name flowers elsewhere and long ago, as girls—
bony knees combing through grass, two different oceans
away. Suddenly I feel misplaced

in this garden; the mulch, warm wind that comes as respite
but isn't. My friend can tell and she assures me,
we are not lost. As proof, she searches

the nearest lamppost's stamped torso, announces
what cross-street can be our fast exit. Her way
of saying, nomatter the thicket,

I will take care of you. After the park, on the east side,
we find one of the reopened bars where the drinks are named
after great American novels. My friend can't *drink drink*

but she urges me to go ahead, choose whatever American story I want,
and I do. Let's splurge, she says, and we order small dishes,
things from the sea: oysters in capers and olives,

ceviche, codfish croquets. When the plates come
she pokes at the passion fruit seeds, jiggly eyes
on the salmon's pink, raw flesh. Is this what we wanted?

She is sweating badly, her hormones rampant. She hadn't been
home home in twenty-three months. She takes in the air, apologizes,
though neither of us is sure what for. We eat and compare

health plans, talk about how and how much we want to be cared for.
If pressed to choose between love and loyalty, I need to promise,
I'll make her take the first. We take turns at the plates.

A swarm of bikers brushes by, leaving behind a tailwind of cheap cologne
and smoke. The waitress checks in, is this what you wanted, girls?
I love that she calls us that, girls. I love how far back

she reaches that way, past everything I'd been seeing us for: two women
landlocked on a small patch of grass too green to be real
at a table the virus had repositioned alarmingly close

to the curb. My friend consigns me the last croquet
and I take it. I take it because we are not lost. And because
this is what we wanted. It must be.

Book of Ruth, *Afterthought*

Because in my own book my story never ends
on the birth of a king.   See, I speak now

a skeptic: how a whole scroll, *a woman's life in it*—
lands on a brief   however foretelling line.

When it arrived, my story's told ending, the beef stew
was on the stove   seething, I remembered

learning the first rule of *shechita*. The blade must move quick
on the throat,   one compassionate sweep

for a lawful transection. The heifer stunned
with its own warm gushing.   Too stunned to know

its own end. It does not sway. It does not twist
the lithe ropes of its form.   Therefore, we say, it is tender.

Author's Notes

A line in "Exodus Song" heavily borrows from a line in Richard Siken's poem "Scheherazade," which opens his book *Crush*: "How it was late, and no one could sleep, the horses running/ until they forget that they are horses."

The Ruth series of poems corresponds with the biblical *Book of Ruth*. The newly-widowed Ruth joins Naomi, her mother-in-law, in migrating from the famine-stricken Moab to Judah. In Hebrew, the name "Ruth" is derived from the word, *reut*, meaning friendship, a name denoting Ruth's loyal friendship to Naomi. Upon the women's migration to Moab, in attempt to secure protection, food, and shelter, Ruth makes herself known (allegedly, sexually) to Boaz, a wealthy landowner, whom she eventually marries. Whereas traditional interpretations of *Book of Ruth* emphasize the friendship between the two women as well as their abidance to the common law and patriarchal tradition in Judah, few modern interpretations suggest an erotic relationship between Ruth and Naomi.

The dictionary definition form of the poems titled, "Ruth \ˈrüth \ *(n.)*" is modeled after Traci Brimhall's poems titled, "1. (n) A colony of rooks," "2. (n) A breeding place," and "3. (n) A crowded Tenement House," which respectively open the three sections of her book, *Rookery*.

The opening of "Lemons from Levant" borrows and slightly alters a line from the poem, "Mahler in New York" by Joseph Fasano, from his book, *Fugue for Other Hands*: "If I carry my father with me, it is the way/ a horse carries autumn in its mane."

"Afloat" is for Lara Payne.

"Campanology" borrows, alters, and corresponds with the opening lines of Mary Oliver's poem "Where Does the Temple Begin, Where Does It End?" in her book *Why I Wake Early*: "There are things you can't reach. But/ you can reach out to them, and all day long./ The wind, the bird flying away. The idea of God."

Founded in 1972 by Father Bruno Hussar, Wahat al-Salam – Neve Shalom (Arabic and Hebrew for *Oasis of Peace*), is a cooperative village of Palestinian and Jewish citizens of Israel, dedicated to promoting peace, justice, and equality. The village was founded on a stretch of no man's land and is situated a symbolically equal distance from Tel Aviv and Jerusalem, as well as from Ramallah according to one source. Its name is derived from the book of Isaiah (32:18), "My people shall dwell in an Oasis of Peace." As part of the village's commitment to co-existence, its civil, cultural, and educational life is conducted bi-lingually in Arabic and Hebrew. Established in 1984, the School for Peace in Wahat al-Salam – Neve Shalom is open to all and offers extensive programming in civil engagement, co-existence, and constructive dialogue. A portion of the proceeds from *Song in Tammuz* will be donated to the Wahat al-Salam – Neve Shalom School for Peace.

"Dirge with Humming Desert" has been poured, at times directly, into the vessel of the poem "What They Found in the Diving Bell" by Traci Brimhall, published in *Poem-a-Day*.

"Lucie Last Summer" borrows and slightly alters a line from Wallace Stevens' poem, "Final Soliloquy of the Interior Paramour." The line reads, "How high that highest candle lights the dark" and proceeds to the poem's final stanza, "Out of this same light, out of the central mind, / We make a dwelling in the evening air, / In which being there together is enough."

"My Grandfather Shows Me the Sepia Photograph Tucked in his Passport Pocket but Does Not Say Auschwitz" borrows its form, with slight alterations, from the poem "Seventh Circle on Earth" by Ocean Vuong, which appears in his book, *Night Sky with Exit Wounds.*

The ending of "Ruth Twelve Years After Crossing the Water" is modeled after the ending of the poem "Mahler in New York" by Joseph Fasano, from his book, *Fugue for Other Hands*: "because it is the way we would like to be carried:/sometimes with mercy, sometimes without."

"She is Three and to Her This is Just the World" is for Alma Rouger-Sternberg.

"Oh You Bruised Your Knee She Says and the Truth is I did Not" is for Dr. Mari Su.

"Ruth on the Third Day of Mourning" is in memory of Hanna Tadmor, with love.

"In Gratitude" is for Elvira Sihvola.

Several poems in this collection, including "Dirge with Humming Desert," "Writing to You," and "Ghazal from an Ocean Away," arise from my experience of growing up in Israel, a country whose history has been shaped by recurring war, violence, grief, and longing. The intuition to write these poems comes from that lived experience alone. They do not presume to speak for the Palestinian experience, which belongs to Palestinian poets and writers to tell. Nearly all of the poems in this collection were written before October 7, 2023. They are not responses to that dark day or to the dark days that have followed. It is my passionate belief that every people deserves to live in peace, security, dignity, and self-determination. My hope is for the day when Israelis and Palestinians alike may live in safety, justice, and freedom, whether in one shared homeland or one alongside the other.

Acknowledgments

Gratitude to the editors of the following journals who had offered first homes to these poems, sometimes in different iterations:

The Adroit Journal
"My Sister Carrying Her Darkness Like Silver"
"Ruth Remembers Imagining the Foreign Field Before Leaving Moab"
"Ruth \ ˈrüth \ *(n.)*"
"Writing to You"
"Campanology"

Beloit Poetry Journal:
"Ruth, *Oil on Canvas, Francesco Hayez, 1835*"

Cider Press Review
"Ruth from a Sudden Clearing in the Foreign Field"

Cincinnati Review
"After the Bad Year I Want Things to Be Still"

Crab Orchard Review
"Ruth Twelve Years after Crossing the Water"

Fugue Journal: "Lemons from Levant"

Iowa Review
"Book of Ruth, *Afterthought*"
"Ruth Before Leaving Moab"
"Night Will Soon Fall on the Lake"
"Ruth \ ˈrüth \ *(n.)*"

The Journal
"Afloat"

Mississippi Review
"In Gratitude"

Narrative Magazine
"My Grandfather Delivers a Survivor's Testimony at Yad Vashem but Does Not Say Auschwitz"

New England Review
"Exodus Song"
"Dirge with Humming Desert"

The New Republic: "In the Tongue I Was Born To"

Ninth Letter: "Oh You Bruised Your Knee She Says and the Truth is I Did Not"

Prairie Schooner
"Ghazal from an Ocean Away"
"Lucie Last Summer"

Six Finch
"Self-Portrait in Virginia, Facing East"

Tupelo Quarterly
"Ruth One Year after Leaving Moab"
"She is Three and to Her this is Just the World"
"Ruth Seeing a Herd of Wild Oryx on a Hill in Jericho"
"My Grandfather Returns to His Birth Town in Now-Slovakia and Remembers the Music"
"Ruth on the Third Day of Mourning"

"My Grandfather Delivers a Survivor's Testimony at Yad Vashem but Does Not Say Auschwitz" was anthologized in *Best New Poets 2024*.

"Nothing Promised" was featured in the Academy of American Poets' *Poem-a-Day*, October 2025.

Gratitudes

Wild fields of gratitude to the brilliant and visionary team at Tupelo Press, especially Jeffrey Levine, Kristina Marie Darling, and David Rossitter. Jeffrey: when you said, *welcome to the Tupelo family*, you meant it. My generation of writers and those to follow have oceans to learn from your principled, humanistic, and open-minded approach to the arts and the art of publishing. Kristina: How you manage to uplift so many literary voices—women especially—all with uncompromising dedication and acumen, remains a mystery to me. To say I admire your literary leadership is an understatement.

To my legendary teachers at Harvard College and the Columbia MFA program: I don't know which has been my greater education— your writing or your teaching. Luckily one does not have to choose. To Henri Cole, for suggesting "a freshness" to what others might have called second language interference. Josh Bell, for introducing me to devotional poetry and inviting me back into the bible stories I'd grown up with, replacing past didacticism with curiosity and wonder. Humility in other words. To Jorie Graham for teaching attention and the wing flaps of birds.

Timothy Donnelly, Dottie Lasky, Alan Gilbert, Robert Ostrom, and Mark Wunderlich: your brilliant teaching and generosity with our poetry cohort has often made me doubt if any class of poets ever did come before or after ours. To Lucie Brock-Broido, tender with our hearts and fierce with our poems. I am still learning to be *less and less embarrassed about more and more.* Your aura is everywhere, though nothing has ever been the same.

To my fellow poets at Columbia, especially Erika Luckert, Nathan Xavier Osorio, Katrine Øgaard Jensen, Patrick Errington, and Isabella DeSendi. Erika and Nathan: the image of you late at night, hand-stitching a poetry chapbook with our cohort's first-year work, says everything about your ingenuity and care for community. It can't speak to each of your immense talent, but I can. Erika: what I've learned from you far exceeds the bounds of poetry or the margins of this page. Thank you.

I am grateful to the conferences, residencies, and workshops that allowed a rare equilibrium between solitude and community through the writing of this book. To my workshop leaders at Bread Loaf: Carl Phillips, Brenda Shaughnessy, and especially Rick Barot—admired poet, teacher, and mentor. Rick, you changed everything. Thank you for lighting my path. To the Vermont Studio Center, Virginia Center for the Creative Arts, Yaddo, Office Hours Poetry Workshop, and Poets & Writers' Publicity Incubator among other programs. The friends and guides I've met in those provided kindness, candidness, and various brands of genius through the writing of this book. Carlene Kucharczyk, Jennifer Manthey, L.A. Johnson, Farnaz Fatemi, Lara Payne, James Fujinami Moore, Laura Creste, Megan Pinto, Sarah Sala, and Lynn Melnick— thank you.

To my teaching colleagues at Columbia and New York Universities, for being proof that teaching and writing don't have to compete, nor do exceptional brilliance and exceptional kindness: Aaron Ritzenberg, Abby Rabinowitz, Vanessa Guida, Sue Mendelsohn, Brian Trimboli, Jason Ueda, Raluca Albu, Suzanne Cope, and Chris Edling.

To Beowulf Sheehan, justly called *a poet working with light*, for the invitation to see myself, and for seeing.

To Peter LaBerge and *The Adroit Journal*: This book and I owe so much of our becoming to your uplift. Thank you for your generosity and belief in the work from early on.

Sagi Frish, among the first children born in Oasis of Peace – Wahat al-Salam – Neve Shalom: thank you for welcoming me to the village amidst the unbearable heat. A remarkable *oasis of hope*.

To my creative sisters and confidants, sometimes across generations: Shira Kogan, Elvira Sihvola, Shoshana Barzel, and Donna Spruijt-Metz. Thank you for your friendship, listening, and so often—perspective. In art and in life: let's keep each other dreaming.

To Savta Debby, for the love of language. Savta Hanna and Gideoni: Nothing of my journey would have been possible without your open-mindedness, love, and unwavering support.

Ima, Aba, Maya, and Ohadi: I left home for overseas so young and on my own. Thank you for the trust you instilled in me, and for your selflessness in letting me go. You receive me upon every return, as I am. Ima and Aba: you are within the breath of every line in this book.
אני אוהבת אתכם

Above all, to Ofir, Tamar, and Romi. You are joy and you are light. You three are the music that transcends all words.

AVIA TADMOR's poems appear in The Academy of American Poets' *Poem-a-Day*, *The New Republic*, *Best New Poets*, *New England Review*, and elsewhere. She received fellowships and awards from Yaddo, Bread Loaf Writers' Workshop—the Rona Jaffe Foundation, the Vermont Studio Center, the Virginia Center for the Creative Arts, and the *Adroit Journal*'s Gregory Djanikian Scholars Program. Previously, Avia taught writing at Columbia University, where she directed the Columbia Artist/Teachers Program, promoting no-cost arts education in schools and community organizations in New York City. A graduate of the United World College program educating for constructive dialogue, peace, and a sustainable future, Avia is a Clinical Associate Professor at New York University. Born in Jerusalem, she lives in New York.

Recent and Selected Titles from Tupelo Press

of Women: 20 Japanese Female Poets / 20 Waka Poems Naoko Fujimoto

AutoPortrait (as flotsam) Kirsten Kaschock

Them That Slept: New and Selected Poems Larissa Szporluk

Other Paths for Shahrazad Jennifer Jean, ed.

Slipstream Diana Cao

The Book of Marys and Glaciers Carrie Olivia Adams

The Andrew Wyeth Chronicles Janée Baugher

Identifying the Pathogen Jennifer Militello

Indifferent Cities Ángel García

Something Small of How to See a River Teresa Dzieglewicz

Force Drift: An Essay in the Epic Jeffrey Pethybridge

Tips to Help You Do Your Best Mike Carlson

Cyborg Fever Laurie Sheck

Daphne Kristen Case

Nebulous Vertigo Belle Ling

Westminster West Chard de Niord

Jalousie Allyson Paty

Mycocosmic Lesley Wheeler

Phantom Number: An Abecedarium for April Spring Ulmer

The Haunting Cate Peebles

The Radiant Lise Goett

The Opening Ritual G.C. Waldrep

The Right Hand Christina Pugh

Called Back Rosa Lane

Landsickness Leigh Lucas

Green Island Liz Countryman

The Beautiful Immunity Karen An-hwei Lee

Small Altars Justin Gardiner

Country Songs for Alice Emma Binder

Asterism Ae Hee Lee

then telling be the antidote Xiao Yue Shan

Therapon Bruce Bond & Dan Beachy-Quick

membery Preeti Kaur Rajpal

How To Live Kelle Groom

Sleep Tight Satellite Carol Guess

THINE Kate Partridge

The Future Will Call You Something Else Natasha Sajé

Night Logic Matthew Gellman

The Unreal City Mike Lala

Wind—Mountain—Oak: Poems of Sappho Dan Beachy-Quick

Tender Machines J. Mae Barizo

Best of Tupelo Quarterly Kristina Marie Darling, ed.

We Are Changed to Deer at the Broken Place Kelly Weber

Why Misread a Cloud Emily Carlson

The Strings Are Lightning and Hold You In Chee Brossy

Ore Choir: The Lava on Iceland Katy Didden and Kevin Tsang

The Air in the Air Behind It Brandon Rushton

www.ingramcontent.com/pod-product-compliance
Lightning Source LLC
LaVergne TN
LVHW070543160926
848142LV00041B/449
* 9 7 8 1 9 6 1 2 0 9 6 9 5 *